HUMANS VS. ARTIFICIAL INTELLIGENCE

by Clara MacCarald

WATSON

www.focusreaders.com

Copyright © 2020 by Focus Readers®, Lake Elmo, MN 55042. All rights reserved. No part of this book may be reproduced or utilized in any form or by any means without written permission from the publisher.

Focus Readers is distributed by North Star Editions:
sales@northstareditions.com | 888-417-0195

Produced for Focus Readers by Red Line Editorial.

Content Consultant: Magy Seif El-Nasr, Associate Professor of Khoury College of Computer Sciences, Northeastern University

Photographs ©: Seth Wenig/AP Images, cover, 1, 28–29, 32; Lee Jin-man/AP Images, 4–5, 7, 9; Tobias Hase/picture-alliance/dpa/AP Images, 11; Everett Historical/Shutterstock Images, 12–13; Rui Vieira/PA Wire URN:7439818/Press Association/AP Images, 15; AP Images, 17; George Widman/AP Images, 18–19; Red Line Editorial, 21, 27 (infographic); Adam Nadel/AP Images, 23; SolisImages/iStockphoto, 24–25; Lemberg Vector studio/Shutterstock Images, 27 (cat); Keith Srakocic/AP Images, 31; Kathy Willens/AP Images, 35; Marie D. De Jesús/Houston Chronicle/AP Images, 36–37; tommaso79/Shutterstock Images, 39; DmyTo/Shutterstock Images, 40–41; yoshi0511/Shutterstock Images, 43; Zapp2Photo/Shutterstock Images, 45

Library of Congress Cataloging-in-Publication Data
Names: MacCarald, Clara, 1979- author.
Title: Humans vs. artificial intelligence / Clara MacCarald.
Other titles: Humans versus artificial intelligence
Description: Lake Elmo, MN : Focus Readers, 2020. | Series: Artificial intelligence | Includes index. | Audience: Grades 7 to 8.
Identifiers: LCCN 2019025657 (print) | LCCN 2019025658 (ebook) | ISBN 9781644930755 (hardcover) | ISBN 9781644931547 (paperback) | ISBN 9781644933121 (pdf) | ISBN 9781644932339 (ebook)
Subjects: LCSH: Artificial intelligence--Competitions--Juvenile literature. | Soft computing--Juvenile literature. | Games--Juvenile literature.
Classification: LCC Q335.4 .M335 2020 (print) | LCC Q335.4 (ebook) | DDC 006.3--dc23
LC record available at https://lccn.loc.gov/2019025657
LC ebook record available at https://lccn.loc.gov/2019025658

Printed in the United States of America
Mankato, MN
012020

ABOUT THE AUTHOR

Clara MacCarald is a freelance writer with a master's degree in biology. She lives with her family in an off-grid house nestled in the forests of central New York. When not parenting her daughter, she spends her time writing nonfiction books for kids.

TABLE OF CONTENTS

CHAPTER 1

HUMAN VS. COMPUTER

On March 9, 2016, Lee Sedol sat down to play the board game Go. Three officials watched from a raised table. Cameras showed the game on television, and more than 60 million people tuned in. Lee was a Go **grandmaster**. He was one of the best players in the world.

Go was first played thousands of years ago in China. Go has simple rules. Players take turns placing stones on a board covered in a grid.

Lee Sedol (right) played Demis Hassabis's computer program in five games of Go in 2016.

The stones go on the points where two lines cross. Stones cannot be moved once they've been placed. To remove the opponent's stones from the board, a player must surround them with his or her own stones. At the end of the game, the winner is usually the player whose stones cover the largest part of the board.

Playing Go is anything but simple. People spend years mastering the game. The number of possible moves in Go is greater than the number of atoms in the universe. Even a computer cannot consider all of these moves.

A man sat opposite Lee during the game. But Lee's actual opponent was a computer program named AlphaGo. The man would merely place the stones according to AlphaGo's instructions. Lee had watched AlphaGo play before. He felt certain he would win with ease.

Lee places the first stone in his first game against AlphaGo. DeepMind programmer Aja Huang watches.

Lee went first. He placed a black stone. Next, AlphaGo placed a white stone. Lee and AlphaGo began taking turns, each player trying to control parts of the board.

AlphaGo was created by computer scientists at DeepMind. Instead of following specific instructions from **programmers**, AlphaGo had taught itself how to play Go. It started by studying more than 10,000 real Go games played between humans. Then it played millions of games against itself. It discovered which moves were more likely to lead to success. It became a better player.

Lee and AlphaGo covered the board with stones. Suddenly, AlphaGo made a move that gave it an unexpected advantage. Shocked, Lee collapsed back into his chair. He considered the board carefully. But the damage had been done.

Lee lost four out of five games against the computer program. AlphaGo won the match. It proved that a computer program could become a Go champion. In one of the world's most complicated games, artificial intelligence (AI) came out on top.

AI is the study and design of computer systems that have human skills such as thinking, reasoning, and understanding language. Some computer scientists define AI as creating systems that mimic the way humans do these things. Others define AI as creating systems that are intelligent themselves.

▲ Lee reviews the board after losing his third game in a row to AlphaGo.

Many experts consider games to be one way to test AI for true intelligence. Intelligence is the ability to not only gain knowledge and skills, but also to apply them. Computers can easily perform math or find facts. But games involve **strategy**, risk-taking, and interactions with an intelligent opponent. And after decades of playing games, computers are gaining the upper hand.

DEEPMIND

In 2010, Demis Hassabis started the company DeepMind with his friends Mustafa Suleyman and Shane Legg. Hassabis had a vision. He wanted to build a computer that could learn anything just by looking at data. But his company began by building programs that could tackle individual games.

In 2014, Google bought DeepMind. Though DeepMind was no longer independent, the company continued to develop AIs. DeepMind researchers created a video game–playing AI called DQN. The researchers trained DQN on 49 classic video games. Methods of play varied by game. For example, DQN might have to fire a shooter, fight with an opponent, or race a car. DQN learned to play all the games as skillfully as a human expert.

DeepMind researchers followed the success of DQN with the creation of AlphaGo. But DeepMind works on other uses for AI beyond game playing. DeepMind AIs have reduced Google's energy use. They have worked to deliver better health care. The DeepMind team has published results from their research in more than 200 papers. Through it all, DeepMind continues to work toward Hassabis's dream of a general AI that can address any problem.

CHAPTER 2

COMPUTERS PLAYING GAMES

In 1946, the US government announced the first electronic, general-use computer. The new machine, named ENIAC, was so large that it filled a room. It took days to program ENIAC to solve a problem. But ENIAC could perform thousands of calculations per second. Scientists imagined the things they could do with that power. Some scientists wondered if one day a computer could become not only powerful, but also intelligent.

ENIAC was 150 feet (46 m) long and covered three walls of a basement room.

Alan Turing was a famous early computer scientist. He was interested in the question of how people could know if a computer was truly thinking. He thought that one way to test AI was through the game of chess. In 1948, Turing started working on a chess-playing program called Turochamp. He gave it instructions on how to play the game. Instructions given to a computer are called algorithms. Turochamp used the algorithms to calculate how best to move. It could consider the possible outcomes of the next two moves. Based on its predictions, it identified the best current move.

In 1950, when Turing finished the Turochamp program, computers weren't strong enough to run it. Turing challenged his friend Alick Glennie to a game anyway. Glennie played normally. Turing played using Turochamp. When it was Turing's

Alan Turing's Bombe machine helped the British crack German military codes during World War II (1939–1945).

move, he looked at the algorithms in order to calculate which move Turochamp would make. Turochamp wasn't a good player. Twenty-nine moves after the game began, Glennie won.

In the following decades, computer programs improved. In 1958, a chess program managed to beat a human player, although not a skilled one. In 1967, a computer played in human chess **tournaments**. It won a few games.

In 1987, students at Carnegie Mellon University created Deep Thought. This **supercomputer** could consider 1.5 million moves per second. In 1988, it became the first chess computer to defeat a grandmaster in a regular tournament. The following year, it smashed the competition at a tournament of chess computers.

That same year, Deep Thought went up against the world chess champion, Garry Kasparov. They played a two-game match in New York City. Deep Thought was actually in Pittsburgh, Pennsylvania. Its programmers had to send its moves by telephone. When the games started, Kasparov quickly took charge. He won both games, to the delight of the spectators.

Meanwhile, a programmer named Jonathan Schaeffer turned to a different game: checkers. He created a program called Chinook. In 1992,

△ Garry Kasparov (right) became the youngest world chess champion after beating Anatoly Karpov in 1985.

Chinook faced off with the world checkers champion, Marion Tinsley. Thirty-three of their games ended in a tie. Chinook won two games and lost four. It lost the overall match but proved that computers could compete in a serious way against humans.

While Schaeffer continued to improve Chinook, other people focused on chess programs. Chess pieces can move in more ways than checkers pieces can. People saw chess as the game to beat.

CHAPTER 3

DEEP THINKING

Even though Deep Thought had lost against Garry Kasparov, computer scientists at the company IBM were impressed. They invited some of Deep Thought's programmers to join an IBM team. The team wanted to create an even more powerful chess-playing supercomputer. Their research resulted in Deep Blue, an updated version of Deep Thought. The new supercomputer could do 100 million calculations per second.

The AI program Deep Blue was created to challenge chess champion Garry Kasparov.

In 1996, the Association for Computing Machinery held a celebration. It had been half a century since the creation of ENIAC. To celebrate, the group invited Deep Blue and Kasparov, who was still the world chess champion. Years before, Kasparov had cheerfully beat Deep Thought. But they had only played two games. This time, human and supercomputer would play as if in a regular tournament. They would follow strict time limits. And they would play a match of six games.

Deep Blue played first. It powered up slowly as a timer counted down, but it finally made its move. The players moved pieces around until Deep Blue began to corner Kasparov. Kasparov tried to mount an attack, but Deep Blue struck back. Seeing his position was helpless, Kasparov **resigned**. Deep Blue had won the game. Accepting his loss, Kasparov shook hands with the programmer playing Deep Blue's moves. But Kasparov was not defeated. He went on to win three games, tie two, and take the match.

Deep Blue's programmers went back to work. They knew they needed to improve Deep Blue before they could hope to beat Kasparov. With the help of other chess grandmasters, they gave the supercomputer a collection of openings to learn.

TOURNAMENT TIME LIMITS ◀

During a regular tournament, players must pay attention to the clock or they risk running out of time and losing the game. The following time limits (set in hours) were used during the 2018 World Chess Championship Match.

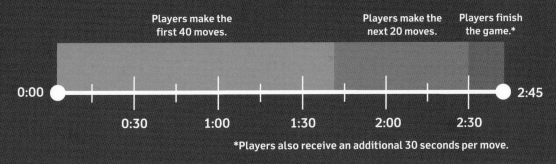

Players make the first 40 moves.   Players make the next 20 moves.   Players finish the game.*

0:00   0:30   1:00   1:30   2:00   2:30   2:45

*Players also receive an additional 30 seconds per move.

Chess openings are the first few moves a person plays. Openings can set the tone for the rest of the game. People have studied standard openings for hundreds of years. They've also studied strategies for dealing with them.

The grandmasters played against Deep Blue. When problems came up, the programmers would add or change the supercomputer's algorithms. Many of the algorithms were added to computer chips called chess chips. The new Deep Blue used 480 chess chips to consider as many as 200 million positions per second.

In 1997, Deep Blue and Kasparov had a rematch in a small television studio in New York City. Millions watched. Kasparov was convinced he would triumph again. But in the first game, a move from Deep Blue surprised him. Some people later thought the move may have resulted from a

▲ Kasparov considers his next move during the second game of his six-game rematch against Deep Blue in 1997.

computer bug. Kasparov recovered and won. But he lost the second game.

Kasparov began to think the programmers were cheating. In the last game, Deep Blue used a clever strategy that shocked him. He felt the strategy required a human mind. Though the game was not over, Kasparov lost the will to fight. He resigned. Deep Blue had won two games, tied three, and lost only one. Deep Blue had beaten the world chess champion.

CHAPTER 4

MACHINE LEARNING

Although games such as chess and Go are difficult, they have rules that programmers can enter into a computer. For example, pieces can only make certain moves. At first, AI relied heavily on the computer's speed. In general, the faster a supercomputer could make its calculations, the better it got. Programmers could also change algorithms based on how well a certain algorithm worked during play.

Computer programmers can alter a program's strategy by changing its algorithms.

But intelligence involves more than just following rules. The real world doesn't always have rules that are easy to understand or learn. In order to compete with human intelligence at a wide range of tasks, AI needed a different approach. Some programmers thought the answer lay in neural networks. Neural networks are groups of algorithms connected in ways that mimic connections in the human brain.

Neural networks can find patterns by grouping together bits of information that seem related. Data enters an AI program. That data goes through layers that each examine a different feature of the data. The AI then gives the data a label. Sometimes its labels don't match the labels a programmer gives. In those cases, the AI can change its approach. Its algorithms shift to get the right answer. It learns to perform better.

Machine learning happens when an AI gains new knowledge or skills by itself without a programmer having to enter new algorithms. With neural nets and machine learning, computers started challenging humans at games far more difficult than chess.

A BASIC NEURAL NETWORK ◄

Neural networks can consider several aspects of something such as a picture and return a single label.

NEURAL NETWORK

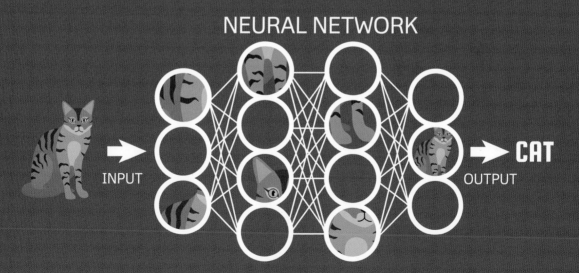

INPUT

OUTPUT

CAT

CHAPTER 5

HUMANS IN JEOPARDY

In the mid-2000s, IBM researchers decided to test AI with the TV quiz show *Jeopardy!* The show's host provides the answer to an unknown question. **Contestants** hit a buzzer when they think they know the question. If contestants are correct, they win money. If they are wrong, they lose money. The winner is the contestant with the most money in the end. In 2007, an IBM team began working on a *Jeopardy!*-playing program.

Alex Trebek is the host of the TV quiz show *Jeopardy!*

Problems popped up right away. Winning the game requires understanding not only basic language, but also tricky uses of language such as jokes. So, focusing on one word in a sentence could mislead a computer. If the AI buzzed in on every single question, it could quickly lose a lot of money by giving wrong answers.

IBM researchers named their supercomputer Watson. It used 90 **servers** and 15 **terabytes** of memory. Just four of these terabytes held 200 million pages of information for Watson to search. Other parts of Watson's memory held 6 million rules of logic. These rules helped it judge problems and make decisions.

Watson practiced against former *Jeopardy!* champions. In just one second, Watson could perform 80 trillion functions. It began by picking out the key words in a clue, such as names or

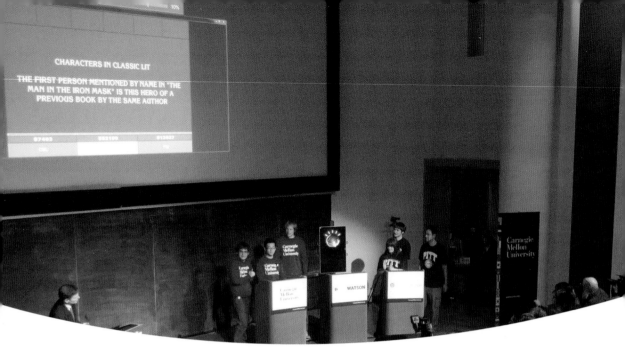

△ Watson competes against university students in 2011.

dates. It then used grammar rules to consider how the words related to one another. Finally, for every clue, it found and ranked hundreds of possible answers. When it found one that had a high enough likelihood of being correct, it buzzed in.

In 2011, Watson played *Jeopardy!* superstars Ken Jennings and Brad Rutter in three games over three days. The two human champions stood on either side of a screen displaying a glowing globe.

▲ Watson beats Ken Jennings and Brad Rutter to the buzzer in a practice round of *Jeopardy!*

The screen represented Watson. But Watson's real work was done in a separate room. During the game, Watson used a device to press a buzzer. The computer gave each answer out loud.

Watson started slow, tying with Rutter the first day. But on the second day, Watson pulled ahead. It buzzed in extremely fast. However, sometimes Watson didn't buzz in at all. It had calculated its response was unlikely to be the correct one.

Watson also made silly mistakes. For example, it responded to a question about a US city with a Canadian one.

Most of the time, though, Watson was able to answer correctly. And in the end, it won the whole match. Its total score was $77,147, compared to the $45,600 won by both humans together.

Jennings made a clever joke about losing. Watson couldn't joke. Unlike the two human contestants, Watson didn't understand what any of its answers actually meant. But the fact that Watson could work with language so well signaled a huge leap forward for AI.

THINK ABOUT IT ◀

Some people thought Watson only won because it was fast on the buzzer. Why would that take away from the impressiveness of Watson's win?

IBM

The International Business Machines (IBM) Corporation formed in 1911. From the beginning, IBM developed and sold machines that dealt with information. IBM products recorded information, processed it, and stored it.

In the 1950s, IBM researchers began working on chess-playing computers. After the success of Deep Blue in 1997, IBM continued to work on supercomputers. In 2004, IBM presented Blue Gene, which could perform 280 trillion calculations per second. Blue Gene supercomputers have helped humans map the human genome and understand climate change.

IBM also continued to improve game-playing AI. All game-playing programs work with change. The pieces move in chess. The questions change in *Jeopardy!* But the rules of the game stay the same. For example, a chessboard never suddenly

▲ In 1999, Dr. Ambuj Goyal presents the computer chip that will power Blue Gene, IBM's new supercomputer.

adds a new row. When the basic rules of a game change, most computers fall apart. They can't apply what they learned from the original game. They must learn the adjusted game from scratch.

But in 2019, IBM announced a leap forward in AI. Its new program played a video game. It learned to fly a bird between pipes without hitting the pipes. When the distance between the pipes changed, the program could adapt its play to the new setup. The ability to adapt will help computers work better in the real world.

▲ People can speak to computer assistants such as Siri and ask questions or give commands.

Beyond analyzing data, Watson could also understand language and answer questions. With its ability to recognize speech, it could act like the popular computer assistants Alexa and Siri. In 2018, IBM introduced Watson Assistant. Like its rivals, Watson could respond to human comments and commands with appropriate actions. IBM programmers had given Watson skills to master a game. Watson could now use those skills to help humans in the real world.

CHAPTER 7

GO TO THE FUTURE

Similar to Watson, AlphaGo used neural networks and machine learning to master the game Go. AlphaGo started with some human strategies. It also studied thousands of real games played by humans. AlphaGo played so well that South Korea's Go Association awarded the program the highest rank given to Go grandmasters. But in 2017, AlphaGo lost to a superior player: AlphaGo Zero.

AlphaGo learned some of its strategies by studying Go games played between humans.

Unlike the original program, AlphaGo Zero learned to play with very little help from humans. DeepMind programmers had only given it the rules of Go to start with. AlphaGo Zero played against itself until it mastered the game.

Programmers celebrated this development. It can take a long time for humans to train a computer program. A program that can learn on its own could tackle much larger problems than chess or Go. It might solve climate change or discover new drugs.

Then DeepMind went beyond even AlphaGo Zero. It created AlphaZero. Programmers could

> THINK ABOUT IT

Why do you think an AI that learned a game all by itself would play better than one that learned from humans?

Shogi is another strategy game similar to chess and Go. AlphaZero defeated the world champion program in 2017.

give the new program the rules of any two-player game. AlphaZero would do the rest. After just a few hours of playing, it would master the game. In December 2017, AlphaZero won or tied every game it played against the current world champion of chess-playing programs, Stockfish. It also mastered shogi, known as Japanese chess, and Go.

As good as game-playing programs have become, humans are still better at some things.

Computers still need people to tell them what problems to address. Deep Blue could never have designed a computer program like itself. Deep Blue could only play chess, which it had been programmed to do. Even AlphaZero only plays the games people tell it to play.

Computers also lack what people call common sense. They have no general knowledge of the world outside what they are told. For example, Watson responded to one *Jeopardy!* question about what grasshoppers eat with a term used for human food. Watson had no way of knowing its answer was not only wrong but also comical. But some AI researchers are working to teach computers common sense. This ability is difficult to teach. It takes a lot of work to identify the many things people know without having to think about, such as that hurting people makes them angry.

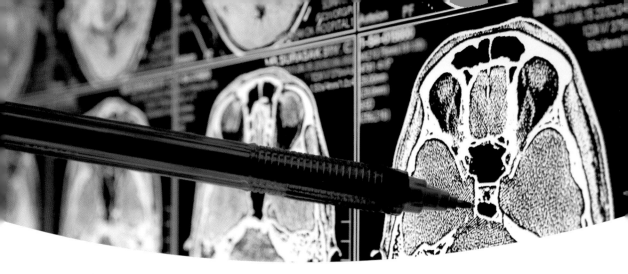

▲ Beyond the world of games, programmers have tested AI for use in medical diagnosis.

The rivalry of humans versus AI continues. But people such as Garry Kasparov think that a rivalry is the wrong way to look at AI. Two decades after losing to Deep Blue, Kasparov promoted the idea of human-computer teams challenging each other to play chess. He believed that in the future, similar teams would improve human lives. For example, they could work in important fields such as medicine. AI may have won in the world of games. But together, humans and AI can create positive change in the real world.

HUMANS VS. ARTIFICIAL INTELLIGENCE

Write your answers on a separate piece of paper.

1. Summarize how Watson became a *Jeopardy!* champion.

2. Do you think that playing a board game is a good test for intelligence? Why or why not?

3. In what year did world chess champion Garry Kasparov lose a match to Deep Blue?

> **A.** 2016
> **B.** 1997
> **C.** 1989

4. What might have happened if programmers gave strategies to AlphaGo Zero rather than let the program learn by playing itself?

> **A.** It would have been a worse player at Go.
> **B.** It would have been a better player of Go.
> **C.** It would have beaten Kasparov at chess.

Answer key on page 48.

GLOSSARY

app
A computer program that completes a task.

contestants
People taking part in a competition.

grandmaster
An expert player with world-class skills.

programmers
People who create, add, or change the instructions in a computer program.

resigned
Gave up on a game by accepting defeat rather than continuing to play.

servers
Computers that make data or programs available to other computers.

strategy
A plan for winning a game.

supercomputer
A powerful computer capable of doing a huge number of calculations very quickly.

terabytes
Collections of approximately one trillion bytes, each of which is a single bit of data.

tournaments
Series of contests between several contestants.

TO LEARN MORE

BOOKS

Hulick, Kathryn. *Artificial Intelligence*. Minneapolis: Abdo Publishing, 2016.

Jackson, Tom. *Will Robots Ever Be Smarter Than Humans? Theories About Artificial Intelligence*. New York: Gareth Stevens Publishing, 2019.

Naber, Therese. *How the Computer Changed History*. Minneapolis: Abdo Publishing, 2016.

NOTE TO EDUCATORS

Visit **www.focusreaders.com** to find lesson plans, activities, links, and other resources related to this title.

INDEX

Answer Key: 1. Answers will vary; **2.** Answers will vary; **3.** B; **4.** A